Drugs and Driving

Activists constructed a mock crash scene to illustrate the dangers of driving while under the influence of drugs and alcohol.

The Drug Abuse Prevention Library

Drugs and Driving

Janet Grosshandler

The Rosen Publishing Group, Inc.
New York

Published in 1992, 1994, 1998, 2001 by the Rosen Publishing
Group, Inc.
29 East 21st Street, New York, NY 10010

Copyright © 1992, 1994, 1998, 2001 by the Rosen Publishing
Group, Inc.

Revised Edition 2001

Library of Congress Cataloging-in-Publication Data
Grosshandler, Janet.
Drugs and Driving/Janet Grosshandler.
(The drug abuse prevention library)
Includes bibliographical references and index.
Summary: Discusses the use of drugs by teenagers, and in par-
ticular, the consequences of combining drugs and driving.
ISBN 0-8239-3459-4
1. Automobile drivers—United States—Drug use—Juvenile liter-
ature. [1. Automobile drivers—Drug use. 2. Drug abuse. 3.
Drinking and traffic accidents. Traffic accidents.]
I. Title II. Series
HE5620.D65G76 1992, 1994
363.1'251—dc21   92-6146
                                                          CIP
                                                           AC

Manufactured in the United States of America

Contents

It Could Be You:
Tom's Story

"I never thought it could happen to me."

It was normal for Tom and his friends to go out drinking and partying on Saturday nights. They lived in a small town out in the country where they rarely encountered another car late at night. Driving around after drinking and smoking a little pot just didn't seem that dangerous. It felt as if they were the only people in town still awake and out on the roads. What could go wrong? But one particular Saturday night, Tom took his partying too far. He endangered his own life, as well as ended the lives of four innocent people, all because he was irresponsible enough to drive under the influence of drugs and alcohol.

"That Saturday, my folks let me take the car out. I picked up my girlfriend,

Four teens drove this car from Vermont into Canada, where the drinking age is only eighteen. On the way home, they all were killed in a drunk driving accident.

Melissa, and drove to Dave's, where he was having a keg party. I downed a few brews and took a hit of grass, and I was feeling pretty good. I just wanted to relax a little, you know?

"It wasn't long before Melissa told me she wanted to leave the party. I guess she could tell I wasn't sober, because she offered to drive my car. But I didn't think that getting behind the wheel would be dangerous. And I didn't want anyone to think I couldn't handle myself, so I told her I was fine. There is something embarrassing about your girlfriend driving you home while you sit in the passenger seat. Or that's what I used to think. I still can't believe how stupid I was. If only I had just let her drive the car, things would have ended differently. I thought I was in absolute control of the car and myself. I thought I was as alert as always. I guess that was the booze and pot talking, because I wasn't in control at all.

"Anyway, we backed out of the driveway and went down Dave's street to the corner where you turn left onto the four-lane. I didn't really stop at the stop sign because it was the middle of the night, and I couldn't see any cars. There are never any cars at that time of night. I didn't look too closely, I guess, because the next thing I remember, there's this van speeding up from the right. Actually, that's the last thing I remember about that night."

Three weeks later, Tom woke up in a hospital bed. He was greeted with the news that he had been in a coma all that time, but even worse, his impaired driving caused four deaths. Melissa, as well as the young couple driving the van and their two-year-old daughter, were killed in the car crash. The cars *collided so hard that both Melissa and the family were killed on impact. Physically, Tom got off relatively easy. After his hospital stay, he had to spend a year doing physical therapy to make his legs work properly again. He still had his life, but it had become haunted by the memory of those whose lives his reckless driving ended.*

Tom doesn't take drinking and driving lightly anymore. He has been convicted of two counts of manslaughter. He has to pay $30,000 in fines and serve ten years of community service. And worst of all, he has to live with the guilt, because he thought he was too cool to admit he was drunk.

"I can never forgive myself for causing Melissa's death or the death of that young family who were just driving down the street, minding their own business and trying to get home. Now I refuse to let my friends drive if they've been drinking or doing drugs or let them take rides from people who are impaired. You just never know what can happen. Believe me, it can happen to anybody."

Overview

Thousands of people every year are killed because a teenager has gotten behind the wheel of an automobile while under the influence of drugs. Alcohol is not the only drug that can affect your driving by slowing your reactions and confusing your judgment. All drugs can. Drugged driving is to blame for the deaths of many innocent people. There's nothing cool about getting high and hitting the road. Your "high" could very well result in crippling injuries, death, and murder charges.

Every year, hundreds of thousands of people are maimed, scarred, paralyzed, burned, and killed in accidents caused by impaired driving. In 1999, according to the National Highway Traffic Safety Administration (NHTSA), 38 percent of all traffic accidents were alcohol-related. That same year, 15,786 people were killed in

Drunk drivers kill and maim thousands of people each year.

alcohol-related accidents, while more than 630,000 were injured. That averages out to about one person killed every half hour and one person injured every minute due to impaired driving. In 1998, there were about 2 alcohol-related traffic deaths per hour, 44 per day, and 306 per week. This is the equivalent of two large airplanes crashing with no survivors every week for a year. Most important for you to know is that on an average weekend, one teen dies per hour in a car crash, and 50 percent of these crashes are alcohol-related. On average, eight young people a day die in drunk-driving accidents.

ALCOHOL IS ONLY PART OF THE STORY

These statistics all relate to alcohol-related accidents. When you think of an accident related to driving under the influence, you probably think of drunk driving. But alcohol is not the only drug that interferes with safe driving. There are many drugs, such as cocaine, marijuana, crack, amphetamines, and barbiturates, that will cause someone to drive poorly. Different drugs have different effects on driving, but you can be sure to experience problems with good judgment, as well as coordination and reflexes, if you get behind the wheel while under the influence of drugs.

Some over-the-counter medicines can affect your driving ability, too. Sleeping pills, cough medicines, allergy pills, cold remedies, and pain relievers may contain ingredients that can interfere with your driving. Read the labels on medicine bottles you have at home. A lot of them contain alcohol and carry warnings not to drive or operate machinery when using them. These medicines may also cause drowsiness, sleeplessness, nervousness, and irritability. Adding just a little bit of alcohol to over-the-counter drugs can make these side effects worse,

Be careful when taking over-the-counter medications: Many contain ingredients that can make you sleepy and unable to drive safely.

increasing your sense of drowsiness, wooziness, and loss of perception. By mixing alcohol and medicine, you may receive a DUI charge even if you've had only one beer.

Remember, in the eyes of the law, ignorance is not an excuse. You are responsible for finding out what your medication contains and how it may affect you. So ask your pharmacist what physical effects to expect from the medicine you buy, and read carefully all labels and packaging that come with any medication. Any drug, including alcohol, can interfere with your vision, your driving skills, and your ability to make safe judgments.

Because they are not experienced drivers, teens cause a disproportionate number of automobile accidents.

THE DANGERS OF TEEN DRIVING

Even if you've never been in a single car accident, that doesn't mean you are any less likely to get into one in the future. Teenagers are especially at risk for accidents, because they do not have years of driving experience under their belts and may react incorrectly to sudden problems on the road. Some teen drivers think it's cool to be a reckless driver and try to impress their friends by speeding, tailgating, taking turns too fast, and passing other cars in oncoming traffic. No one will be impressed if you get a ticket, lose your license, or crack up your car, and you will feel like an idiot. And if you hurt or kill someone else while trying to be cool, you will feel terrible and regret it for the rest of your life.

As a new driver, your chances of getting into an accident are high. In fact, 80 percent of fatal accidents are caused by drivers who have never been in a single car accident before. Add drugs to this equation and your chances of getting into an accident dramatically increase. According to Mothers Against Drunk Driving (MADD), teen drivers are responsible for 13 percent of fatal alcohol-related crashes even though they make up only 6.7 percent of the total number of licensed drivers.

Don't be lulled into a false sense of security by telling yourself that you're a good driver. You may be a good driver, but drugs and alcohol will make the best driver an uncoordinated menace. And even if you are a great driver, you have to watch out for the bad drivers out there who may hit you. New drivers should always be especially careful driving and should use good judgment when deciding if they're all right to drive. After all, it's better to spend a Saturday night sober than make a mistake that could cost you your own life, or someone else's.

CRIME AND PUNISHMENT

The penalties for drugged driving are severe. If you are convicted of driving under the influence of drugs, expect your life to change drastically. You will be expected to pay extremely large fines, which can be in the hundreds of thousands of dollars. You can expect many hours of community service ahead of you. You can also expect to have your driver's license taken away, as well as have your insurance company cancel your policy. It will be extremely difficult to find another insurance company that will be willing to take you on unless you pay an enormous amount in premiums. Without insurance, you can't drive. One DUI charge may keep you out of the driver's seat for years. Worse yet—far worse—if you are unfortunate enough to hurt or kill someone while driving under the influence of drugs, you can expect to be charged with a felony, which means you'll be facing jail time (possibly lengthy) if convicted.

You should know that more and more people are being arrested and sentenced to jail time for DUI, even if no one was harmed as a result of the impaired driving. In 1997, according to NHTSA statistics, 1.4 million

Law enforcement agencies often set up roadblocks to catch motorists who drink and drive.

people were arrested for DUI, making it the most frequently committed crime in the United States and the most common violent crime. For DUI offenders sentenced to jail time that year, about 513,200 people in total, the average sentence was six months. Your youth won't get you off the hook, either. Between 1984 and 1993, arrests of teenagers for DUI rose 50.2 percent. Cops are cracking down on teen impaired driving. The days are over when it was treated as a minor mistake in judgment or a harmless youthful indiscretion. Driving under the influence has serious consequences that will affect your life for years to come.

If you intend to party with your friends, make plans to sleep over, take a taxi or bus home, or designate someone who will remain sober and give everyone a ride home.

Chapter

What Drugs Do to You

The things you put into your body will affect the way it functions. For example, eating nutritious foods will make your body healthier than it would be if you ate lots of junk food. Drugs and alcohol are toxic—like poison—so putting them in your body will make you sick.

Drug and alcohol abuse is a serious epidemic! It's been proven that 15 percent of young adults between the ages of twelve and seventeen have serious drug or alcohol problems. That's almost one out of every six teens. If this were a potentially fatal disease, like cancer, and your chances of getting it were one in six, the country would be in a panic. Drug and alcohol abuse can lead to disease, however—the disease of addiction. There is no such thing as harmless experimentation. Drinking alcohol and taking drugs always opens up the door to possible addiction, even if you're doing it for the first time. As a teenager, if you begin experimenting with drugs or alcohol, you will have a 5 percent chance of developing a serious addiction later in life. Once a person is addicted, he or she will feel depressed or sick without the drug. Recovering will be a long and difficult process.

DRUGS AND THEIR EFFECTS

Different drugs affect people differently. But any drug, whether it's illegal, prescription, or over-the-counter, can slow your reaction time, alter your perception of objects around you, make you hyperactive, reduce your peripheral vision (what you see out of the corners of your eyes), or lead to confusion and drowsiness. These side effects will affect your driving skills and make driving very dangerous.

ALCOHOL

Alcohol can kill you, yet many young people don't realize how dangerous it can be. The Center for Substance Abuse and Prevention reports that 2.6 million teenagers aren't aware that alcohol consumption can be fatal. Just as with drugs, you can overdose on alcohol. In fact, hundreds of college students die from alcohol poisoning every year. Alcohol poisoning occurs when a person consumes more alcohol than his or her body can handle, and it is a very serious condition. If you're lucky enough to make it to the hospital to get your stomach pumped, you may survive. But if you're not aware or knowledgeable enough to recognize the signs and get help, your night of partying with friends could have a tragic end.

Alcohol affects many different bodily functions. While drinking alcohol, you'll experience slurred speech, problems seeing straight, and mood swings. Your coordination, judgment, memory, and reflexes will all be impaired. You may even become unconscious or pass out. Obviously, you won't be in any condition to be driving a car.

HALLUCINOGENS

Hallucinogens are drugs that alter your perceptions and make you lose your ability to distinguish between what is real and what is imagined. The sensations you experience may range from feeling high or euphoric (like being detached) to seeing, hearing, and sensing things that are not really there. Because they alter your senses, driving under the influence of hallucinogens involves a very dangerous, reckless attempt to guess what you are really seeing in front of you. It is the equivalent of driving a car while deep in the midst of a

Marijuana can help relieve pain in the terminally ill, but when used without controls, pot can be very destructive.

dream. If you are on these drugs while driving, you may find yourself waking to a nightmare.

Marijuana

Marijuana is a mild hallucinogen that used to be thought of as harmless. In the 1960s, many people experimented with it freely, believing that it didn't have health risks. People also believed that there were health benefits to smoking marijuana. For the most part, research has proven otherwise (though in some states it is legally prescribed as a painkiller and an appetite booster for terminally ill patients). It can have damaging effects on your lungs, just as cigarettes do. It also impairs brain function, so that memory, thought, and the ability to learn and reason are negatively affected. Ironically, when high on pot, some people may emotionally withdraw from their friends and become quiet and depressed. They might also be scared by what's going on around them.

Because marijuana lingers in your body, it can impair your coordination and judgment for several days, long after the high has worn off. A study at Stanford University had airline pilots smoke weak, government-issued marijuana cigarettes, and then tested them on computerized flight simulators. Many pilots crashed their simulated planes right after the marijuana use. More alarming, many of these pilots crashed their simulated planes twenty-four hours later, when they all reported feeling no lingering effects from the marijuana and said they had no worries about flying!

Despite the well-documented side effects— the serious damage to the way your brain works—many young people continue to experiment with marijuana. For many young people, it is the first illegal drug they try after using legal drugs, such as tobacco and alcohol. Some drug experts feel that marijuana acts as a "gateway" drug, leading to the use of harder drugs like cocaine, ecstasy, and LSD.

Marijuana stays in your body and can impair your judgment long after the high is gone, as pilots discovered in studies using flight simulators.

PCP

Another hallucinogen is phencyclidine, known as PCP or angel dust. In small doses, PCP has effects like those of alcohol: poor coordination, slurred speech, mental confusion, sleepiness, and numbness in fingers and toes. Users may also tend to feel nauseated and may vomit.

In large doses, PCP can act like an anesthetic, a drug used to put people to sleep before an operation. Your senses may be disturbed or dulled. Because your senses are muffled, PCP can make you feel cut off from the world and the people around you. It may make you feel left out, alone, and isolated. Some people have felt these effects last up to ten days. PCP can also cause terrible depression, severe mental suffering, or flashbacks. People have even died from taking PCP.

LSD

LSD, or acid, is another hallucinogen. Even in tiny doses, LSD causes the pupils of your eyes to dilate, your blood pressure to rise, your heart to beat irregularly, and the muscles of your internal organs to contract. At first, the effects are slow and mild, but then the hallucinations start. Soon you will begin to think that you can "see" sounds or "hear" colors.

Being on LSD makes you lose touch with reality. That might sound like a good time, until it actually starts to happen. Then it's scary, like being trapped in a funhouse. You may see and hear things that aren't really there. Everything can become distorted and confusing. And a person on LSD will often react to what they think they are seeing happening around them, sometimes resulting in inappropriate and even violent behavior. This can be extremely dangerous, because users can take their ordinarily hidden and controlled violent feelings out on themselves and others. If you become frightened, you can't make these disturbing images and sounds go away. It's a nightmare you won't wake up from anytime soon. An LSD trip lasts for hours, and if a person is having a "bad trip," they will just have to suffer through it till the end.

The effects of LSD aren't over when the trip ends. LSD can stay in your body for years and become reactivated, causing an unexpected drug flashback years later. Imagine how scary and confusing it would be to start tripping again when you're at work, on a crowded subway, or playing with your children.

STIMULANTS

Stimulant drugs speed up the activities of the cells in the central nervous system. They suppress your appetite and boost your mood. The effect is only temporary, however, and the user will end up more tired and low than when he or she started. Caffeine, found in coffee, tea, and soda, and the nicotine found in cigarettes, are examples of stimulants that occur naturally in plants.

Amphetamines

Other stimulants are artificial. They are called amphetamines and were once used to treat certain illnesses, such as depression and obesity. People who are driving long distances

Some hallucinogens may make you see things that aren't there, and may cause you to become frightened and violent.

or studying late will often take them to stay awake and get a quick energy burst. Amphetamines affect your body by speeding up your heart rate and other body functions. You feel excitable, and your speech is fast and unclear. You are restless, and your hands shake. You may perspire and experience sleeplessness. A user may experience other effects such as nervousness, memory lapse, irritability, or hallucination. Headache, dizziness, and blurred vision are also possible. This is why driving after taking an amphetamine is a terrible idea. Your body may be getting a boost, but the brain that controls it is still fatigued and can perceive things incorrectly and make very bad decisions. If you are too tired to drive, take a nap, not a pill.

Ecstasy

One amphetamine that is very popular with teenagers now is ecstasy. It is often used by teens who attend all-night rave parties in which trance-inducing music, dancing, and high-tech light shows all contribute to a "trippy" ambience. Ecstasy users claim it makes them feel euphoric, peaceful, emotionally uninhibited, and very clear-headed. But the side effects can be serious and sometimes devastating. Milder side effects can include

Ecstasy is popular at rave parties, but it contains chemicals that can permanently damage your brain. It is also illegal.

nausea, paranoia, anxiety, blurred vision, increased heart rate and blood pressure, fainting, chills, and convulsions. The more serious consequences include dehydration and dangerously elevated body temperature (which have resulted in numerous deaths nationwide), hallucinations, depression, violent behavior, brain damage, long-term blurred vision, memory loss, and cardiac arrest.

NARCOTICS

Narcotics are drugs that cause sleep or sluggishness and also relieve pain. These drugs are usually made from opium, which comes from the poppy flower. Codeine and morphine are narcotics that are sometimes used as painkillers by hospitals to treat people when they are sick. All narcotics that come from opium or are human-made, like Demerol, can be addictive if abused. That means that your body always craves more of the drug. These drugs slow down your respiratory system. Your oxygen intake can become so low that you die.

Cocaine and Heroin

Cocaine is a narcotic that acts like a stimulant. It is made from the leaves of coca bushes. It makes a person feel sped up and jittery. In large doses, it can make a person hallucinate and get panicked. When cocaine is snorted or injected, the effects on the central nervous system are immediate. The user's heart rate will speed up. The person will begin to breathe much faster and body temperature will rise.

Some people take cocaine for the "rush," that immediate sense of high energy, euphoria, and clear thinking. The rush, however, will last for only about half an hour and leave the user feeling very tired and low, maybe even depressed. Plus, the more you take it, the larger quantities you need to get that rush. Heavy users often become more aggressive and anxious. Mood swings and

Chronic cocaine abuse can cause users to become aggressive and violent.

memory loss have also been reported. Habitual coke users may experience convulsions, and some become paralyzed.

Crack is the street name given to a form of cocaine that is smoked. It looks like small white rocks. Crack is sold in small bottles, in folding papers, or in tinfoil. It is usually smoked in a pipe. Crack is an extremely addictive drug.

Heroin is a narcotic that can be taken in several ways. In pure powder form, it can be smoked, snorted into the nose through a straw or rolled-up dollar bill, "skin popped" (injected just under the skin), or "mainlined" (injected directly into the vein). It is one of the most addictive drugs on Earth.

SEDATIVES

Sedatives are another class of drug that affect the central nervous system, but in the opposite way that stimulants do. Sedatives slow down the body's functioning, so the user's blood pressure, heart rate, breathing, and cell function drop. If the quantity of sedatives taken is too high and these bodily activities slow down too much, the result is life-threatening.

Barbiturates are sedatives that are used to treat certain medical problems, such as epilepsy, insomnia, anxiety disorders, and alcohol and heroin withdrawals. They are often used to relax some patients before and during surgery. Unfortunately, these drugs seem to be over-prescribed. They can become habit-forming. If you take barbiturates, your reactions and responses are slowed, your speech is slurred and mixed up, and you feel sluggish. Your thinking becomes muddled. An overdose can cause death.

If you become involved with any of these drugs, you take risks with all aspects of your life—your health, your mental stability, your family, your relationships, your present, and your future.

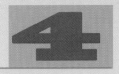
Facts About a Growing Problem

Think about these statistics provided by MADD:

✔ Every weekday night from 10 PM to 1 AM, one in thirteen drivers is drunk. Between 1 AM and 6 AM on weekend mornings, one in seven drivers is drunk.

✔ In 1997, 21 percent of young drivers involved in fatal car accidents had been drinking. Almost 25 percent of those arrested for DUI each year are under the age of twenty-five.

33

✔ One out of three teenage deaths is due to a car accident. In fact, traffic crashes are the leading single cause of death for every age from birth through age thirty-three. Almost half of these fatalities are alcohol-related.

✔ In 1996, one in four high school sophomores and one out of three seniors reported they had had five or more alcoholic drinks, at one occasion, within the past two weeks.

✔ Teens who drink alcohol are 7.5 times more likely to use other drugs and 50 times more likely to use cocaine than teen nondrinkers.

✔ In 1999, 55 percent of high school seniors admitted that they had used an illegal substance.

Drinking and taking drugs can strain your relationships with your friends and loved ones.

GOING WITH THE CROWD

Depending on your crowd, your friends may not drink, may drink once in a while, or may drink often and push drinking as a requirement to stay in the crowd. While giving into peer pressure to drink or take drugs may create a temporary peace with your friends, it will almost certainly lead to fights with your parents and boyfriend or girlfriend, a slide in your grades, health problems, and trouble with the law. You will also be putting yourself into possibly life-threatening situations, such as overdoses and car accidents. Are the people who are encouraging you to make this trade-off really your friends? Would a friend really ask you to place your relationships, health, and life in jeopardy?

WHY DO PEOPLE DRIVE UNDER THE INFLUENCE?

Overconfidence

A couple of drinks or a few hits of pot can affect someone's judgment, causing him or her to forget about consequences, confuse the taking of dangerous risks with fun and excitement, and be overconfident in his or her abilities. Some people think they can drive better when

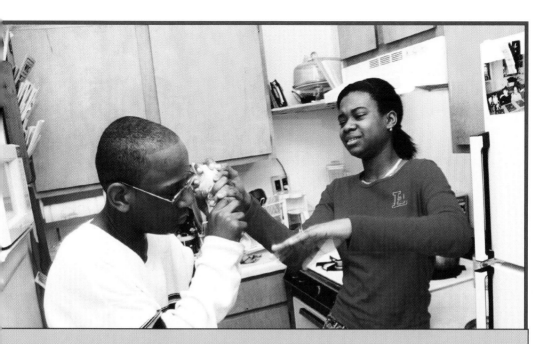

If you've had too much to drink at a party, it's better to let a friend call a cab than to risk your life and the lives of others by driving drunk.

drunk or high. This is a physical impossibility; your skills can only get worse under the influence of drugs.

Rationalization

To excuse impaired driving, people will often tell themselves that home is only five minutes away, or no one is out on the road right now, or they've done this hundreds of times before and never had a problem. But it takes only one car to pull out in front of you, one pedestrian to jaywalk, one cyclist with no reflectors, or one moment of drowsiness to change your life forever because you didn't have the driving skills necessary to react quickly and properly.

Fear

It's not easy to call your parents and ask to be picked up because you drank or smoked too much. It's also very hard to admit you are too out of it to drive. It doesn't seem cool to have your parents pick you up at a party, or have to sleep over at someone's house because you went a little too far. It's almost as hard to speak up to try to keep an impaired friend from driving. It might make you feel like a killjoy or a nag. These fears are what allow people to drive under the influence. Just remember, staying alive is cool. Driving under the influence or letting someone else do so is as uncool as it gets.

Poor Planning

A lot of people go to a party knowing that they are going to drink or take drugs, but don't bother to arrange for a place to stay or a sober friend to take them home. When the party is over, their judgment has been affected by what they've consumed. If they try to drive themselves home, this is a disaster in the making. If you plan to party, plan also to sleep over, call a taxi, take the bus, or get a ride home from a designated driver.

What Can Drugs Do to a Driver's Skills?

Drugs interfere with many skills that a person needs to be a safe driver. *Reaction time* is how quickly you respond to something. Slamming on your brakes, pulling to the side of the road to avoid hitting a car, or honking your horn all take a split second to do. Drugs such as alcohol and barbiturates slow down your ability to perceive and understand what's going on around you. Drugs take away that split-second ability to see, decide, and react, making an accident difficult to avoid.

Peripheral vision is the ability to see things that are not right in front of you, but at the side of your vision. Billboards, houses, other cars, and street signs pass on both sides when you are cruising down the road. You need to be able to see when another car pulls out of a driveway or intersection, or when the car next to you pulls up to change lanes.

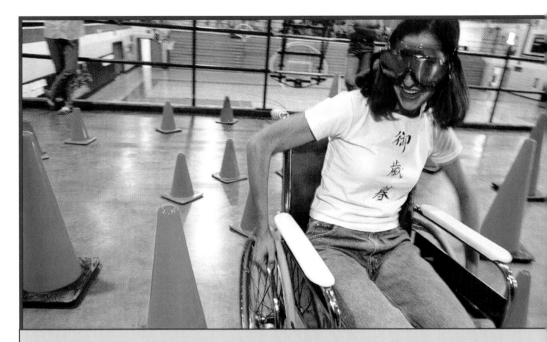

A student wears goggles and pilots a wheelchair through an obstacle course in an exercise that simulates alcohol's effects on vision and balance.

A person with a blood-alcohol content (BAC) of .55 (only one or two drinks in two hours for most people) loses almost one-third of peripheral vision on a field-of-vision test. Your speed also affects peripheral vision. The faster you go, the more blurred your peripheral vision becomes, and the less able you are to see things off to the side.

Divided attention is the ability to pay attention to several things at the same time. When you are driving, your brain must react to all of the things you see in front of you. Think about it: Between traffic lights, street signs, merging and exiting traffic, passing cars, steering, fiddling with the radio and turn signals, the glare of the sun or the lights of oncoming vehicles, there are dozens of things to which you must pay attention and react. Drugs and alcohol make it far more difficult to pay attention to several things at once.

Night vision is your ability to see when it is dark. Driving at night requires even more caution and concentration than daytime driving. This is because at night, your vision can be reduced by as much as half. Taking drugs, especially alcohol, reduces the oxygen in your bloodstream, which affects your vision. Then you drive with even less night vision than when you are sober.

Tracking skills are what allow you to guide your car along the curves of a road. Drugs and alcohol affect your brain's tracking skills, leading to an inability to follow curves and stay in your lane. This is why drunk drivers swerve along the road.

But I'm Not a Criminal! Drugs and the Law

If you drive under the influence of drugs, you are a criminal. That may not seem fair, but think about it. A person who is high doesn't have the mental and physical control he or she needs to drive a car. And a car that isn't in control can become a lethal weapon at any moment. You are operating a very heavy machine that is hurtling through space at speeds as high as fifty miles an hour or more. That is an enormous responsibility and an even more enormous danger under the best of circumstances. Operating a vehicle when drunk turns the already risky activity of driving into criminally reckless behavior. The laws against DWI (driving while intoxicated) and DUI (driving under the influence) are in place to protect innocent people from getting hurt or killed by a driver who's not in control.

42

Students must take—and pass—a Breathalyzer test before they are admitted to the prom at Grant High School in Grant, Nebraska.

IF YOU ARE PULLED OVER

If you are pulled over because a police officer suspects you of DUI, you will be asked to do some things to determine whether or not you are drunk. Your blood-alcohol content (BAC) will be tested with a Breathalyzer. You may also have to take a coordination test, doing things such as walking a straight line and touching your nose. If you refuse to cooperate, your license can be suspended for thirty days.

If your breath measures .10 or higher on the Breathalyzer, you are legally drunk or intoxicated. In some states, a reading between .05 and .10 means that you are legally impaired. You could then be taken to a hospital for urine and blood tests.

But what if the Breathalyzer says that you are not drunk from alcohol, yet other drugs have impaired your ability to drive a vehicle? If you are suspected of driving while high, you may be taken to a trained drug recognition tester, who will put you through tests to see if you're clean. You'll be tested for such things as the reaction of your pupils to light, the speed of your pulse, quivering eyelids, bloodshot eyes, muscle rigidity (from PCP use), and needle scars. The recognition tests cover seven categories of drugs: (1) central nervous system depressants (like alcohol); (2) stimulants (cocaine, amphetamines); (3) hallucinogens (LSD); (4) narcotics (heroin, Demerol, codeine); (5) PCP and similar drugs; (6) marijuana and hashish; and (7) inhalants (glue, etc.).

CONVICTION

If you are convicted in court of DUI, you'll pay heavily for it. And if you are found to be both drunk and high, you can be convicted of two separate crimes at once. The punishment for driving while using illegal drugs is much stricter than for driving drunk.

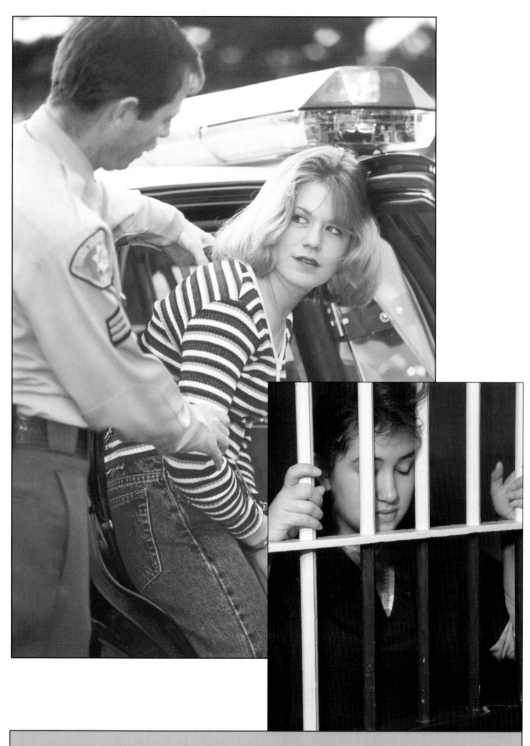

Driving under the influence can ruin your life in many ways: You could be arrested and go to jail, or even kill someone.

Fines

The laws differ in each state. In the states of Indiana and Washington, for instance, you may have to pay a fine of up to $5,000.

Jail

In states such as Washington, there's a minimum of twenty-four consecutive hours that you'll be stuck in jail, and a maximum period of one year. In Delaware, the minimum is sixty days, while the maximum is six months.

Seizure of Your Vehicle

For a second DUI offense, states such as Tennessee have a law that allows the state to take your vehicle away.

Rehabilitation

If you are convicted of a DUI, you may have to go through a driver improvement program. Many states also make you go through a local alcohol or drug rehabilitation program to help you straighten out your drug problem.

Probation

Instead of jail time, some states put you on probation for one to three years. A probation officer checks with your family, school, and job to make sure you are staying sober. And you have to report to your probation officer at specific times.

License Revocation

Getting a driver's license feels like the beginning of adult freedom, but it's also the beginning of adult responsibility. If you are convicted of DUI, you will lose your license for at least a few months and possibly as long as two years. You will give up your freedom because you neglected your responsibility.

Money Problems

It's expensive to pay a lawyer to defend you. Add to that the court costs and the fines you'll receive, and you've suddenly got one hefty bill.

Job Loss

Employers don't want employees they cannot rely on. And if you can't get to work because you have no license or car, you'll most likely be deemed unreliable. Plus, try getting a job with a criminal conviction on your record. Most job applications ask if you've ever been convicted of a crime. Few employers feel comfortable hiring someone who has been convicted of impaired driving. Rightly or wrongly, you just won't come across as trustworthy.

Preventing a Tragedy

If you use drugs and then get behind the wheel, the consequences can be fatal. You can kill innocent people, your own friends, or yourself. Just over half of Americans killed in impaired-driving accidents were the impaired drivers themselves. Twenty percent of those killed were the passengers of impaired drivers, and 17 percent were innocent pedestrians and cyclists caught in the wrong place at the wrong time. An additional 6 percent of those killed were sober drivers unable to get out of the way of out-of-control impaired drivers.

Laurie was driving her friend home after a daytime wine and cheese party that she and her high school band friends had organized at a

Even a couple of glasses of wine with friends can lead to a fatal accident if you drive after you drink.

student's house whose parents were away. This wasn't any keg party, and it was broad daylight, so she just didn't think drinking two glasses of wine would seriously affect her. Taking the turn into her friend's neighborhood far too fast, she crashed into a telephone pole. Laurie's leg and arm were crushed. Her college music scholarship is now in jeopardy. And her best friend is dead.

Jess is paralyzed from the waist down—the result of an almost lethal combination of cocaine and his friend's motorcycle. "I had offered to give him a ride home because I knew he was a little too cranked up to ride. But he said he had never let anyone else ride his motorcycle, and he had no intention of being a passenger on his own bike. He said he was way more alert on coke anyway; it actually improved his driving. So I agreed. But I should have listened to my instincts. Then I could be riding a motorcycle instead of being stuck in this wheelchair."

Randi was a straight-A student and president of her senior class. In September, she was going off to college to major in philosophy. A seventeen-year-old driver high on marijuana changed her life forever. Serious injuries from a car accident left Randi a paraplegic with contracted and spastic hands and feet. She is also brain-damaged and can speak and make herself understood only with great difficulty. She can no longer write. She will never leave her wheel-chair. Randi was the innocent victim of another person's bad decisions.

WHAT YOU CAN DO

So what can be done to prevent similar tragedies from happening in your town and to people you care about? The first thing you can do to protect the lives of people in your community is to vow never to get behind the wheel of a car when you are impaired and to try to prevent your friends or family members from doing so, too. By trying to ensure that your immediate circle of friends and family always drives safely, you will already have done much both to protect your loved ones and make your town's streets safer. There are other ways, however, for you to extend this good influence to more and more people in your community. Here are some of them:

PROJECT GRADUATION

Project Graduation is a national alcohol-safety program designed to keep kids safe, healthy, and alive during prom and graduation time. Participants in this program:

- ✔ **Have teens sign pledges not to drink or do drugs and drive.**
- ✔ **Set up a Safe Rides system.**
- ✔ **Promote a "Buckle-Up Day."**

If you know that you will be drinking, hire a limo or a car service to drive you around. It's worth the expense.

SADD

Students Against Destructive Decisions (formerly Students Against Drunk Driving) are groups of high school students who want to do something about the deadly combination of drinking and driving. In 1981, Robert Anastas, director of health education in the Wayland public schools in Massachusetts, organized the program in his schools. The idea spread quickly.

CONTRACT WITH PARENTS

In this SADD program, teens and parents sign a contract in which they both agree to be responsible for the teen's safety. The teen agrees that he or she will always ride with a sober driver and buckle his or her seat belt. If teens are in dangerous situations, they also agree to contact their parents to pick them up. The parent agrees that he or she will pick up the teen at any time, day or night, no questions asked.

SAFE RIDES FOR TEENS

Many schools have a Safe Rides program. If you or your ride home is drunk, you can call Safe Rides for a trip home. It is usually run by students, parents, teachers, and other volunteers. If you don't have a Safe Rides program at your school, speak with your teacher or principal to get one started. You might also ask a service organization in your town to work with you on the project.

ORGANIZE AN ASSEMBLY

Put on an assembly with speakers who have had drunk-driving tragedies or schoolmates who have lost a friend or relative to drugs and driving. Plan for the police or safety commission to do a car-crash demonstration. Have a persuasive speaker convince the

Mothers Against Drunk Driving sponsors candlelight vigils for the friends and relatives of those killed in drunk-driving accidents.

attendees to take a pledge to stand up for their own lives and the right to be safe when they drive.

PEER COUNSELING

Peer counseling means students helping each other. It uses students as role models, helpers, and leaders. Pairing up older, responsible teens with younger ones who need help, information, a contact, or a good influence is usually successful.

CONCLUSION

Do you sometimes feel that you have no power, that you can't change the world? You may say, "I'm only one person. What can I do?"

There is a lot you can do right in your own little corner of the world. Working with a branch of SADD, helping students get safe rides, and being a role model can all make a difference.

It can save a life, including your own.

Glossary

alcoholic Of or containing alcohol; a person suffering from alcoholism.

anesthetic Drug used in surgery to numb the sense of feeling.

barbiturate Any of the various drugs used as sedatives, or to make a person sleep.

consequence Result or outcome.

euphoric Feeling relaxed; happy.

felony A serious crime.

flashback A hallucination that occurs long after the initial effects of a drug have stopped.

hallucinogen Drug or chemical that causes hallucinations or distorted experiences.

inhibition Feelings that hold back certain behaviors.

intoxication To be drunk or high on drugs, resulting in reduced mental and physical control.

manslaughter   The accidental, or unintentional, killing of another person.

marijuana   The dried leaves and flowers of the hemp plant; a drug that is smoked.

narcotic   A drug such as morphine or heroin that dulls one's feelings and lessens pain.

rehabilitation   Process of bringing back to a normal or healthy condition.

sedative   Tending to calm.

solvent   A substance that can dissolve another substance.

stimulant   A drug that excites or quickens the body's functioning.

Where to Go for Help

Alcoholics Anonymous
Grand Central Station
P.O. Box 459
New York, NY 10163
(212) 870-3400
Web site:
    http://www.alcoholics-anonymous.org

Center for Substance Abuse Prevention
(800) 662-HELP (4357)

Mothers Against Drunk Driving (MADD)
P.O. Box 541688
Dallas, TX 75354-1688
(800) GET-MADD (438-6233)
Web site: http://www.madd.org

Narcotics Anonymous (NA)
P.O. Box 9999
Van Nuys, CA 91409
(818) 773-9999
Web site: http://www.na.org

The National Council on Alcoholism and
    Drug Dependence
20 Exchange Place, Suite 2902
New York, NY 10005-3201
(800) NCA-CALL (622-2255)
Web site: http://www.ncadd.org

Students Against Destructive Decisions (SADD)
P.O. Box 800
Marlboro, MA 01752
(800) 787-5777

IN CANADA

Alcoholics Anonymous
Intergroup Office, Suite 202
234 Eglinton Avenue East
Toronto, ON M4P IK5
(416) 487-5591

Mothers Against Drunk Driving (MADD)
    Canada
6507C Mississauga Road
Mississauga, ON L5N 1A6
(800) 665-6233
Web site: http://www.madd.ca

Narcotics Anonymous
(416) 236-8956

For Further Reading

Aaseng, Nathan. *Teens and Drunk Driving*. San Diego, CA: Lucent Books, 2000.

Adint, Victor. *Drugs and Prison.* Rev. ed. New York: The Rosen Publishing Group, Inc., 1997.

Dupont, Robert L. *Getting Tough on Gateway Drugs.* Washington, DC: American Psychiatric Press, 1988.

Edwards, Gabrielle I. *Coping with Drug Abuse*. Rev. ed. New York: The Rosen Publishing Group, Inc., 1990.

Grosshandler, Janet. *Coping with Drinking and Driving.* Rev. ed. New York: The Rosen Publishing Group, Inc., 1997.

Grosshandler, Janet. *Working Together Against Drinking and Driving.* Rev. ed. New York: The Rosen Publishing Group, Inc., 1996.

Hicks, John. *Drug Addiction: "No Way I'm an Addict."* Brookfield, CT: Millbrook Press, 1997.

Masline, Shelagh Ryan. *Drug Abuse and Teens.* Springfield, NJ: Enslow, 2000.

Miller, Andrew. *Alcohol and Your Liver: The Incredibly Disgusting Story.* New York: The Rosen Publishing Group, Inc., 2000.

Miner, Jane Claypool. *Alcohol and You.* 3rd ed. New York: Franklin Watts, 1997.

Plant, Martin, and Moira Plant. *Risk-Takers: Alcohol, Drugs, Sex, and Youth.* New York: Routledge, 1992.

Stanley, Debbie. *Marijuana and Your Lungs: The Incredibly Disgusting Story.* New York: The Rosen Publishing Group, Inc., 2000.

Taylor, Barbara. *Everything You Need to Know About Alcohol.* Rev. ed. New York: The Rosen Publishing Group, Inc., 1999.

Index

ABOUT THE AUTHOR

Janet Grosshandler is a guidance counselor at Jackson Memorial High School in Jackson, New Jersey. She earned a B.A. from Trenton State College (now called The College of New Jersey) and followed soon after with an M.Ed. while teaching seventh-grade English.

Coping with Verbal Abuse, *Coping with Drinking and Driving*, *Coping with Alcohol Abuse*, and *The Value of Generosity* are her other books published by the Rosen Publishing Group. Grosshandler lives with her husband and three sons, Nate, Jeff, and Mike, in New Jersey.

PHOTO CREDITS

Cover by Maura Boruchow; pp. 2, 7, 17, 29, 43 © AP/Worldwide; p. 11 © Citizen Patriot/AP/Worldwide; pp. 13, 14, 18, 22, 35 by Maura Boruchow; p. 24 © *The Albuquerque Journal*/AP/Worldwide; pp. 27, 37, 49 by Ira Fox; p. 31 © Malcolm Piers/Image Bank; p. 40 © *The Daily Times*/AP/Worldwide; p. 45 top © S.W. Productions/Index Stock; p. 45 bottom © Dennis Macdonald/Index Stock; p. 52 © Bob Winsett/Index Stock; p. 54 © *The Tennessean*/AP/Worldwide.